The Library of Explorers and Exploration

JACQUES MARQUETTE
and
LOUIS JOLLIET
Explorers of the Mississippi

Tanya Larkin

the rosen publishing group's
rosen
central

Published in 2004 by The Rosen Publishing Group, Inc.
29 East 21st Street, New York, NY 10010

Copyright © 2004 by The Rosen Publishing Group, Inc.

First Edition

Library of Congress Cataloging-in-Publication Data

Larkin, Tanya.
Jacques Marquette and Louis Jolliet: explorers of the Mississippi /
Tanya Larkin.
   p. cm. — (The library of explorers and exploration)
Summary: A biography of the French explorers whose primary goal
was to find the Northwest Passage, but who made their mark on
history by exploring and charting the Mississippi River.
Includes bibliographical references (p.) and index.
ISBN 0-8239-3625-2 (library binding)
1. Marquette, Jacques, 1637–1675—Juvenile literature. 2. Joliet,
Louis, 1645–1700—Juvenile literature. 3. Mississippi River Valley—
Discovery and exploration—French—Juvenile literature. 4. Mississippi
River Valley—History—To 1803—Juvenile literature. 5. Explorers—
America—Biography—Juvenile literature. 6. Explorers—France—
Biography—Juvenile literature. [1. Marquette, Jacques, 1637–1675.
2. Joliet, Louis, 1645–1700. 3. Mississippi River—Discovery and
exploration. 4. Explorers.]
I. Title: Jacques Marquette and Louis Jolliet. II. Title. III. Series.
F352 .L43 2003
                                    2002001213

Manufactured in the United States of America

CONTENTS

INTRODUCTION

THE GREAT RIVER SEEKERS

B efore Robert La Salle claimed the Mississippi Valley for France, before France sold much of that territory to the United States in the Louisiana Purchase, before Mark Twain ever wrote about the Mississippi River, and before anyone gave it the nickname Old Man River, two men from New France (France's colony in Canada) became the first Europeans to seek out and explore the great river. With the approval of King Louis XIV and his officials in the mother country of France, the young colony of New France sent Father Jacques Marquette and Louis Jolliet to explore what the Indians called the Mesippi, or "Great River."

Jacques Marquette was a Catholic missionary and Louis Jolliet was a French-Canadian trader. Both were also explorers, and together they found the waters of the Mississippi River and were the first Europeans to follow the course of the mighty waterway. This sculpture of the two explorers with their Native American guides hangs above the Chicago River in Chicago, Illinois.

In 1673, the French-born missionary, Jacques Marquette, and the Canadian-born fur trader, Louis Jolliet, braved the dangerous rapids of the upper Mississippi and met many different Indian tribes along the way. Most Indians were friendly and welcoming, but others were hostile and threatening. Between the natural dangers of the river and the aggressive Indians who lived on its banks, Jolliet and Marquette narrowly escaped with their lives. The two explorers had different reasons for willingly taking such risks. Father Marquette was spurred on by his spiritual ambition, while Jolliet had more materialistic concerns. Marquette wanted to find Indians who would accept his teachings about Jesus Christ, and Jolliet wanted to expand his fur trade.

The two Frenchmen lived during a thrilling period in European history. Most of western Europe was busy dispatching explorers to every corner of the globe. Exotic foreign goods—such as spices and furs—suddenly flooded the marketplace and became a part of people's daily lives; maps were continuously revised and redrawn; and there was always talk of the discovery of new lands and bodies of water. Marquette and Jolliet were among the many explorers who were caught up in the race to find the most famous body of water of all—the Northwest Passage. It was rumored that this mysterious waterway cut through the North American continent and connected the Atlantic and Pacific Oceans. If such a river, or chain of lakes and rivers, existed, the European trading route to China and Japan would be greatly shortened. The two French explorers may have had different goals at the beginning of their journey. Nonetheless, they shared a common dream. Both secretly hoped that the Mississippi would turn out to be the Northwest Passage to the Southern Sea. The Pacific Ocean was known as the Southern Sea because it was first accessed by crossing the Isthmus of Panama from north to south.

The story of Marquette and Jolliet is a story of disappointment, determination, and ultimate success. The Mississippi did not lead to the Southern Sea, nor was it the Northwest Passage to China and Japan. But other explorers built on what Marquette and Jolliet found out about the course of the Mississippi. Without Marquette and Jolliet's voyage, Robert La Salle would have never had the opportunity to take possession of the Mississippi and its surrounding lands for France, and France would have had a much smaller role in the early development of the United States.

1

THE COLONY OF NEW FRANCE

We have witnessed a notable change in the appearance of Canada. We can assert that it is no longer that forbidding and frost-bound land which was formerly painted in so unfavourable colors, but a veritable New France—not only in the salubrity of its climate and fertility of its soil, but in the other conveniences of life, which are being revealed more and more each day.
— Father François Le Mercier, superior of the Jesuit mission in New France (1653–1656, 1665–1671), from the *Jesuit Relations* of 1666–1667

The French-born missionary, Jacques Marquette, and the Canadian-born fur trader, Louis Jolliet, were among the many explorers caught up in the race to find the most famous body of water of all—the Northwest Passage. As it stood, ships could either sail westward across the Atlantic Ocean and round the tip

Marquette and Jolliet followed in the footsteps of English explorer Henry Hudson, who founded the Hudson River Valley but failed to accomplish what obsessed him the most: finding the Northwest Passage to Asia. Hudson is seen here being greeted by native peoples as he lands at the shores of a lake.

of South America to reach the Pacific Ocean, or sail in the opposite direction around the southern tip of Africa.

The Forgotten Colony

Jacques Marquette was born in Laon, France, in 1637, and Louis Jolliet was born in 1645 in Quebec, New France—what is now Quebec City.

At the time that Jolliet and Marquette were born, the French government had abandoned its desire to find the Northwest Passage; the French no longer cared about expanding their territory or developing their colony in Canada. Samuel de Champlain, who founded New France in the

Before Quebec Was Quebec

Some of the Indian names for Canadian towns remain to this day, while others have been lost. The Indian name for Quebec was Kebec, and Canada's came from the native word Canaga. But Montreal was named by the French—Mont Réal, or Mount Royal. Montreal now stands on the site of what was once an Iroquois settlement called Hochelaga.

Hochelaga, seen here in a map from 1609, was a large Iroquois village with cornfields and a population of 3,000. When the French explorer Jacques Cartier first traveled the St. Lawrence River in Canada in 1535, there were Iroquois living in at least eleven villages between Stadacona (now Quebec City) and Hochelaga (now Montreal). Hochelaga was still there during Cartier's second visit in 1541, but when the French returned to the area in 1603, it and the other Iroquois villages on the St. Lawrence had disappeared.

early 1600s, would have been disappointed. New France's mother country had forgotten it. By the time Jolliet and Marquette were born, the colony had been neglected for years. Many colonists—who had uprooted their families from France and moved to Canada in the hope of making more money—had become disenchanted with frontier life. Part of the problem was the Company of the One Hundred Associates. Though the Company had agreed to develop and protect the colony in exchange for control of all of New France's trade, it did not live up to the agreement.

The Company of the One Hundred Associates

In 1627, Cardinal Richelieu, the prime minister of France since 1624, organized 100 trade leaders into the Company of the One Hundred Associates. The Company promised to populate New France with 4,000 settlers over a period of fifteen years. All new settlers were to work for the Company for three years, and during those years the Company was supposed to support them.

For many years, the French traded peacefully with the native peoples of New France. That changed when the Iroquois began raiding French colonies and killing colonists and other native peoples, including the Hurons, the Algonquins, and the Montagnais.

The residents of Quebec and of the nearby towns of Trois Rivieres, Montreal, and Cap-de-Madeleine, had come to rely on the success of the beaver, martin, and raccoon fur trade. Very few people bothered with the difficult work of clearing the forests to farm the land or got involved with shipping. Instead, the Company of the One Hundred Associates and the Quebecois (people from Quebec) who were expected to work for the Company waited for seasonal trading fairs. During these fairs, tribes such as the Papinchois, the Porcupines,

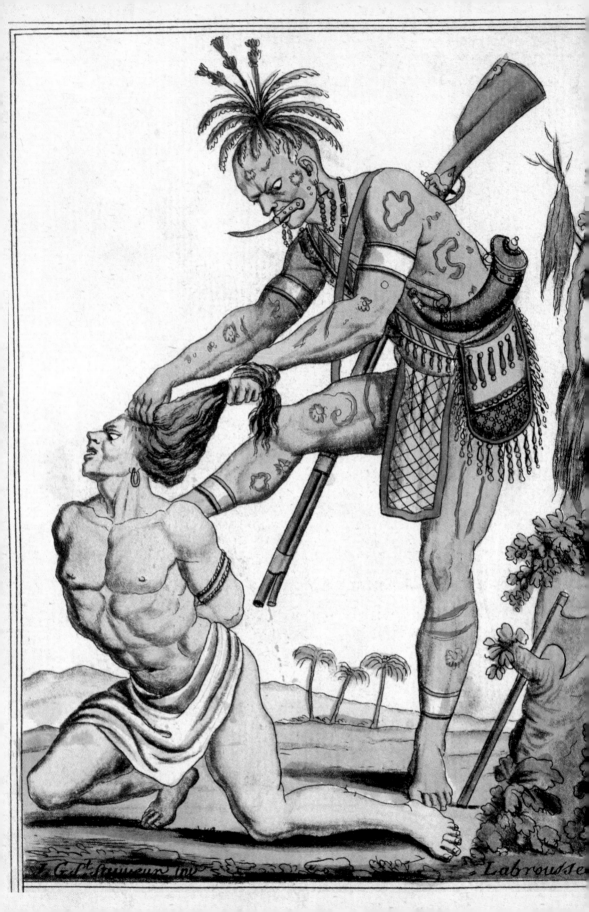

the Bersiamites, and the Montagnais came to the towns on the St. Lawrence River to trade their furs for European goods such as guns, knives, cloth, and glass beads. The Indians especially liked French brandy, which was called *eau-de-vie*, or "water of life." The Frenchmen preferred the Indians' soft, expertly treated pelts to the hard pelts that they might have hunted for themselves.

The Iroquois Attack

Business with the Indians began to fail when the Iroquois started raiding and murdering French colonists and neighboring tribes such as the Hurons, the Algonquins, and the Montagnais. These same tribes would not risk death at the hands of the Iroquois to travel miles to the trade fairs. And when trade with the Indians dried up, the Company of the One Hundred Associates was on the verge of bankruptcy. The French colonists blamed the Company for being unable to provide for them or protect them from Iroquois attacks.

An Iroquois prepares to scalp a man in this illustration. Some historical records indicate that scalping originated among certain Native American tribes, most notably the Iroquois. European settlers in the New World actually encouraged scalping by paying bounties for scalps. According to historical records, the French would pay thirty francs worth of trade goods for a scalp. Their purpose was to encourage the Iroquois to take as many scalps as they could, effectively saving the French the work of killing other tribes.

For so long, the colonists had depended on the surrounding wilderness for lumber, maple sugar, and fur. But suddenly, the wilderness had become a threat to their survival. The dark, boundless woods kept the hostile Iroquois under cover. To make matters worse, the nearby English settlers, who wanted to drive out the French, were supportive of the Iroquois attacks and spurred them on.

The *Coureurs de Bois'* Struggle to Survive

Walking through the ramshackle, dirt streets of Quebec, past the log cabins and a few stone houses, one could sense New France's hopelessness and fear. With the exception of a few brave men, like Louis Jolliet, the colonists wanted to go back to France where they would be safe and life would be easier. Louis Jolliet was a *coureur de bois*, or woods runner. The woods runners of New France did not give up the struggle for survival. They risked their lives by penetrating the wilderness alone to hunt and gather pelts for themselves or to find friendly Indians to trade with. However, they could never go back: The colonists needed the king's permission to return to France and he refused to give it.

Cardinal Richelieu was born Armand Jean du Plessis in Paris on September 9, 1585. He took the name Richelieu from the name of his family's estate. During his service as prime minister he helped France become the leading power in Europe. He supported the French navy and the establishment of French colonies in Africa and the Caribbean.

Back in France, King Louis XIII and Cardinal Richelieu continued to rule together. At the time, a cardinal could be in charge of both war strategy and spiritual affairs. The Catholic Church and the monarchy cooperated on many important issues. Often, however, the Church and the monarchy wrestled with one another for power. Though at times the French were displeased with the underhanded politics of both church and state, they were intensely devoted to God, Jesus Christ, and the Virgin Mary. Many Frenchmen had been educated by Jesuit priests who had dedicated their lives to teaching young boys how to become disciplined Christian adults.

2
PARALLEL LIVES COME TOGETHER

I approach his Paternity to ask that which I sought nearly seven years ago from our deceased Reverend Father General, offering myself in every way, with the consent of superiors, that he order me to set out to foreign nations, about which I have been thinking from my earliest years and the first light of reason, so that I wished to go, even earlier than I was aware. I now believe that there is no safer way for me to gain my end [i.e., of becoming a saint].

—Jacques Marquette in a 1665 letter to the Jesuit
general John Paul Oliva, from Father Joseph
Donnelly's biography of Father Marquette

Marquette and Jolliet lived continents apart—Marquette in a well-established town in France known as a center for religious studies and home to the Cathedral of Notre Dame, and Jolliet in Quebec, New France, which was then, along with Montreal, known as the western frontier of Canada. Though Marquette and Jolliet lived in remarkably different settings—Marquette in a bustling, medieval, walled town on the top of a hill in Laon, France, and Jolliet in Quebec, New

At the age of seventeen, Jacques Marquette entered the Society of Jesus. After twelve years of study and teaching in the Jesuit colleges of France, he was sent to work in the Indian missions in New France in 1666. He worked in Quebec, where he devoted himself to the study of the Huron language. Marquette was soon able to speak six different Huron dialects fluently.

France, a rugged village with unpaved streets and wooden houses bordered by vast woodlands—they both came from wealthy families and ended up following similar paths. Marquette's family served France as soldiers and civil servants as late as the 1700s; many Marquettes sacrificed their lives helping the United States fight England for independence during the American Revolution. Jolliet's family was equally prestigious: Jean Nicolet (an ancestor of Jolliet's) had explored Indian territory as far west as Green Bay, Wisconsin, while searching for China for Samuel de Champlain, the founder of New France. Marquette and Jolliet would pick up where Nicolet left off, going further south of Green Bay in search of a passage to China.

In addition to coming from distinguished families, both men had wanted to be priests from an early age. They were both schooled by Jesuit priests who undoubtedly had a hand in guiding their faith. The Jesuits are a unique order of Catholic priests who dedicate their lives to teaching children and young adults. As a child, Marquette had dreamed of becoming not only a Jesuit priest, like his teachers, but a missionary priest, who would be sent around the world to convert to Christianity those who did not know the teachings of Christ. When he was seventeen years old he was on his way to achieving his dreams: He finally became a Jesuit priest.

21

St. Francis Xavier and the Missionary Calling

In the 1600s it was common for Christians to think that those who did not believe in Christ would burn in hell once they died. Missionaries wanted to save people from hellfire so they went on missions trying to convert people. One such missionary, Saint Francis Xavier, was Jacques Marquette's hero when he was a boy. Saint Francis was called the Apostle of the Indies because he built missions all over India and Southeast Asia in the mid 1500s. He was on his way to China when he fell sick with fever and died.

As a young Jesuit priest, Marquette asked for permission to travel to the Far East, but, in 1659, his wish was denied. The Jesuit superiors may have sensed that he wanted to become a missionary more out of the spirit of adventure than from a genuine desire to spread the teachings of Jesus. By 1665, Marquette had curbed his obsession with the Far East. Father Joseph Donnelly includes a letter from Marquette to his superior Father John Paul Oliva in his biography of the French missionary. Marquette wrote: "I was, once, more inclined to the Indies, but now am completely ready for absolutely any region . . ." In 1666, Marquette was sent to Quebec. Because there were fewer Iroquois attacks, the Jesuits renewed their hope of converting them along with tribes like the Ottawa and Huron, who lived to the

This is an eighteenth-century painting of Saint Francis Xavier. Saint Francis worked primarily in Asia and his first mission was in India, where he landed in 1542. From there he went on to Southeast Asia and established a mission in Japan. He died on his way to the Chinese mainland in 1552. Catholics regard Saint Francis as the greatest missionary since the time of the Apostles. He was canonized in 1622.

west. For years, the missionaries could not travel through the dangerous Iroquois territory to reach the western tribes. Now, they asked France to send more missionaries.

A year after Marquette arrived in New France, Jolliet left the priesthood. This is where the two explorers' parallel lives begin to fork. Jolliet was twenty-three years old when he quit the priesthood. It is not known why he did so. Perhaps he lost his faith, or perhaps the life of a coureur de bois was more appealing. Throughout

23

L. Jollies

their childhood, Louis Jolliet and his older brother, Adrien, played in the wilderness, pretending they were "fur men." They caught fish and hunted small game for their pelts along the St. Maurice River, a small river that empties into the St. Lawrence River at the town of Trois Rivieres. They dreamed of exploring unknown lands. Perhaps these childhood dreams nagged at Louis Jolliet while he was a priest. His brother had become a coureur du bois and had set up a fur warehouse in Sault Ste. Marie on Lake Michigan, which was then known as the Lake of the Illinois.

Kidnapped by the Iroquois

Louis Jolliet admired his brother in much the same way as Marquette admired St. Francis Xavier. When Louis was a teenager, his brother Adrien got lost in the forest and was kidnapped by the Iroquois. Louis knew that his brother could take care of himself in the woods: Adrien knew how to follow the trails of dear and elk, how to orient himself by the position of the sun in the sky, where to find beaver lodges and the best berry patches, and even how to fashion a canoe out of birch bark,

This portrait of Louis Jolliet features his signature. Jolliet was born in New France in 1645. After showing an initial interest in the priesthood, he decided to enter the fur trade near Quebec, the main industry in New France at the time. Jolliet also traveled to France, where he studied hydrography (charting bodies of water) and cartography.

like the Woodland Indians. But after weeks had gone by, the Jolliet family became extremely worried. There was a very good chance that Adrien had been tortured or killed. The Iroquois were infamous for their methods of torture. Adrien eventually returned. That he survived months of captivity in the woods, and also learned the Iroquois language, made him a hero in the eyes of his brother and other French colonists.

Jolliet Goes to France

In 1668, Jolliet left Quebec for France with a loan from Bishop Laval, his teacher at the Jesuit seminary, to study cartography and hydrography with the famous cartographer Jean-Baptiste Franquelin. Jolliet was preparing himself for the life of a professional explorer. While Jolliet was in France, Marquette was busy trying to convert the Ottawa and Huron at Sault Ste. Marie to Christianity. Located along the St. Mary River, which connects Lake Superior and Lake Huron, Sault Ste. Marie was strategically located so that the missionaries could preach to as many tribes as possible. The Chippewas lived at Sault Ste. Marie and were the only tribe who knew how to catch the white fish that poured through rapids. They thrust rods with nets tied onto them into the water and caught six or seven fish at a time in the netted pouches.

Many tribes of Chippewa Indians lived along the Sault Ste. Marie during Jolliet's time in Canada. This drawing depicts Chippewa building a lodge house in 1791.

When Jolliet returned from France in 1668, he outfitted himself in Quebec before heading west to join his brother in the fur trade at Sault Ste. Marie. Jolliet bought a hat, two pairs of shoes, and goods that he and his brother could trade with the Indians, including two guns, two pistols, six packets of rassades (glass beads), twenty-four axes, a gross of small bells, twelve ells of Iroquois-style cloth, six packages of wampum, and forty ounces of tobacco. According to historians, it's possible that Jolliet and Marquette met in Sault Ste.

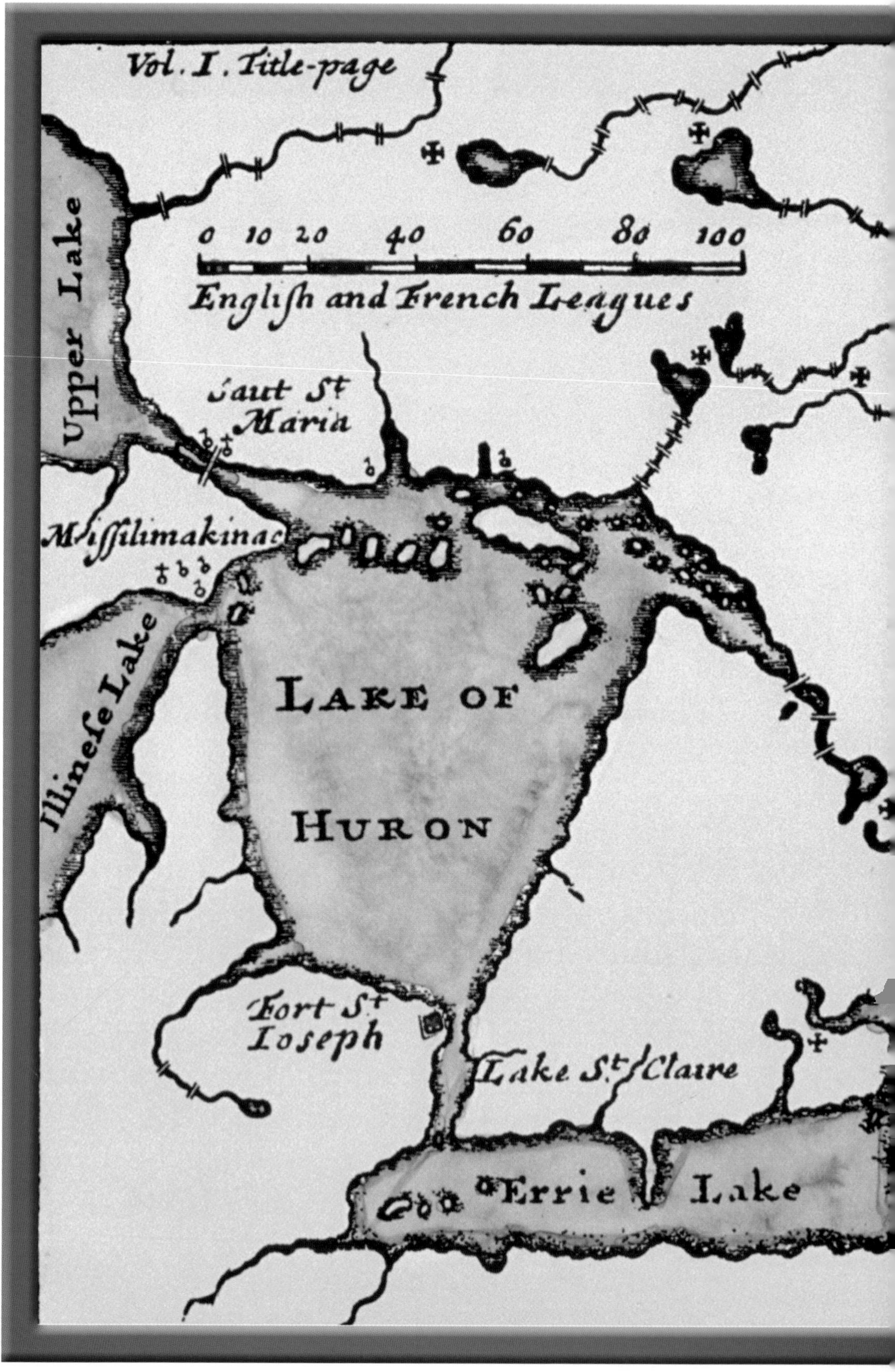
Vol. I. Title-page
0 10 20 40 60 80 100
English and French Leagues
Upper Lake
Saut St Maria
Missilimakinac
Illinese Lake
Lake of Huron
Fort St Ioseph
Lake St Claire
Errie Lake

ark for the Savage Villages
and Carriage
French Settlements

Tado-ussak

Quebec

Mou. Notre Dame

Trois Riviere or
the Three Rivers

Monreal

River of St. Laurence

Champlain Lake

Fort
atenac

ake

tenac

Famine R.

LAND OF THE

Agnies

Onnontagues

Onnoyoute

IROQUOIS

Goyogoans

NEW

Boston

ENGLAND

New
York

Long I.

This map of the Great Lakes and Saint Lawrence Valley was
drawn in 1703. The French and other Europeans, driven by
colonial ambition and religious zeal, dominated the exploration
and cartography of North America in the seventeenth century.

Marie in 1669, before Marquette left to work among the Ottawa and the Huron at the mission of Saint-Esprit on Chequamegon Bay, located at the western end of Lake Superior. It's also possible that they met around 1671, when Marquette returned to Sault Ste. Marie to rest before venturing on another mission on the Straits of Mackinac. Jolliet was in Sault Ste. Marie from the summer of 1669 until the summer of 1671. He was present there when Simon François Daumont, the sieur (sir) of Saint-Lusson, under the intendant Jean Talon's orders, took formal possession of the western areas for Louis XIV and France.

3

RUMORS OF A
GREAT RIVER

On June 4, 1671, the Sieur of St. Lusson, in the name of Louis XIV, took possession of " . . . Sainte–Marie–du–Sault, Lake Huron, Lake Superior, Manitoulin Island, and all of the rest of the country with its rivers, lakes, the rivers and lakes contiguous and adjacent, and their tributaries, as well those discovered as to be discovered, bounded on the one side by the northern and western seas and on the other by the South Sea, this land, in all its length and breadth. Vive le Roi!"
—From *The Jesuit Relations,* LV, 115

What did Marquette and Jolliet talk about when they met? Perhaps Jolliet expressed his desire to carry on the dreams he and his brother had of exploring unknown lands. It's possible that Jolliet looked to Marquette as a brother. Jolliet's brother Adrien had disappeared again in the wilderness, but this time he never returned. Perhaps Marquette confided in Jolliet and told him about his dream of founding a mission among the Illinois tribe. The Illinois had asked Father Marquette

to come and preach to them. The missionaries thought that the Illinois were easier to convert to Christianity than other tribes because they worshiped one spirit that was the creator of all things, like the Christian god.

Tribes Mention the Great River

Father Allouez, Marquette's superior and friend, first met the Illinois at the Saint-Esprit mission on Chequamegon Bay. It was the Illinois who first told Father Allouez that they had to cross a great river before reaching Saint-Esprit. From what Allouez understood from the Illinois, this great river emptied into the sea somewhere near the English colony of Virginia. Soon after, Allouez came into contact with the Sioux. They told him that they lived near the great river named Mississippi. This was the first time Frenchmen had heard the name of the Mississippi River.

Different tribes had spoken to the Jesuits of a great river, and curiosity grew about where it led. Father Dablon, who was the head of missions in the Northwest, had been told of a big river that lay west of the St. Xavier mission—now Green Bay,

It was from the Illinois people he met that Father Marquette first heard tales of the "Great River" (the Mississippi). He realized from talking to them that the river probably emptied into the Gulf of Mexico. He left with the Illinois and set up a chapel on the Straits of Mackinac. It was here that Jolliet later joined him before they set off to explore the river together.

Wisconsin—and ran from north to south. Dablon gathered all of the information about this great river from his priests who worked with the Indians. He concluded that this river either led southwest to the Western Sea or south to the Gulf of Mexico. If it flowed west, it would bring the French to the western side of the Spanish territories. If it flowed south to the Gulf of Mexico, France could prevent the Spanish colony in Florida, and the English colony on the eastern seaboard, from expanding westward. In any case, this river was of extreme strategic importance to France as it could help them gain power over the Spanish and English.

Dablon urged the government of New France to sponsor an expedition down this river. A new government was in place that cared about expanding New France's territory. In 1663, King Louis XIV

The Origin of the Word "Mississippi"

The name "Mississippi" comes from the Algonquian word Missisepe and means "Great River." Missi means "great," and sepe means "river." Every tribe from the Chesapeake Bay to the St. Lawrence River, and west to the Mississippi and Lake Superior (except for the Huron and the Iroquois), spoke Algonquian or an Algonquian-based language.

Although King Louis XIV of France inherited his throne in 1647 at the age of four, he had little actual power until Prime Minister Cardinal Mazarin died in 1661. Known as the Sun King, Louis XIV is remembered for his absolute rule, his patronage of the arts, and the extravagant palace he built in Versailles. Here he is shown holding the plans for that palace.

got rid of the Company of the One Hundred Associates because it had stopped making enough money to support New France and didn't send the king enough profits. The king declared New France a crown land—in other words, a land that was directly under his control—and named Jean-Baptiste Colbert the minister of the colony. Alexandre de Prouville, the marquis de Tracy, was named the lieutenant-general, and Daniel de Remy, the sieur de Courcelles, became the governor.

Jean Talon was the intendant of New France from 1665 to 1668 and from 1670 to 1672. Talon's duties were to rule over New France and serve as minister of justice and finance. He established a royal shipyard and encouraged the search for iron, copper, and other minerals. Talon also convinced the colonists to grow flax and weave their own linen cloth. On his return to France, he was awarded the title le Comte d'Orsainville by Louis XIV.

Talon: A Powerful Leader

Jean Talon became the intendant, which was the name given to the governor's assistant. Fiercely ambitious and extremely capable, Talon was in charge of running the French colonial government. Talon immediately got to work setting New France back on its feet again. He knew that if the colonists used all of New France's resources, they would become rich. Talon started new businesses such as commercial fishing, logging, ship building, sheep raising, and textile manufacturing. He also started a tannery and a brewery, and he encouraged exploration.

Jean Talon's enthusiasm helped make exploration of the West possible, and so did an uninterrupted stretch of peace between the French and the Iroquois. After suffering a crushing defeat by the French in 1667, the Iroquois signed a peace treaty that lasted eighteen years. The wilderness suddenly became less dangerous.

In 1669, Courcelles, the governor of New France, sent out his first expedition in search of the great western river that led to the sea. Courcelles gave Robert La Salle permission to search for the Ohio River, which, according to the Iroquois, emptied into the sea. In 1672, La Salle had still not returned and Talon's patience was wearing thin. Talon persuaded the new governor and successor of Courcelles, Comte de Frontenac, to sponsor exploration of the Mississippi. He hoped that the Mississippi River would prove to be the Great River of the West.

Frontenac was looking for someone to lead the expedition and Louis Jolliet was a natural choice. He possessed an uncommon mixture of skills. Not only was he a native frontiersman who knew several Ottawa dialects, but he was also an excellent, well-educated mapmaker, and he knew how to use a compass and an astrolabe as well. Jolliet had a good reputation among the Indians, too. The Indians sensed that he had grown up on their turf and trusted him more than they would trust explorers who came from France.

The government of New France did not have the budget to give Jolliet any money for the expedition. Instead they gave him trading rights to all of the regions he would travel through. Though Talon thought he was doing Jolliet a favor by giving him these rights, Jolliet knew better. Exploring was a full-time job. There would be no time to trade with the Indians and no space in the canoes to carry back furs. Jolliet knew that he would have to pay for supplies out of his own pocket and that there was little chance that he would ever make back any of this money. In a moment that some would say was impractical or foolish, Jolliet put aside thoughts of his financial future and gladly accepted the opportunity to accomplish his dreams.

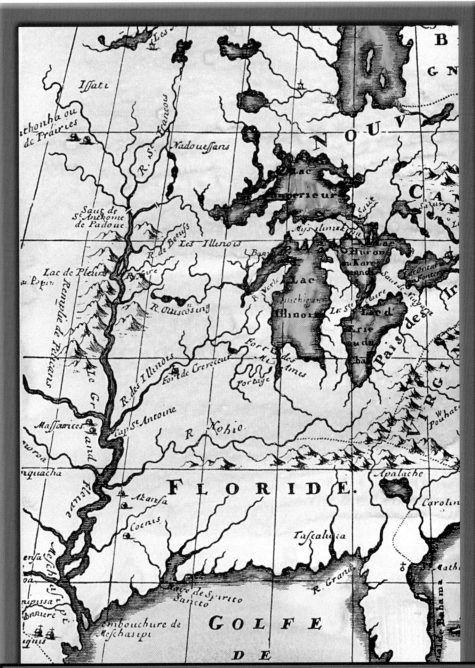

This map of the Mississippi River, Gulf Coast, and Great Lakes region was drawn in 1697 by French Franciscan missionary and explorer Louis Hennepin. He explored the Great Lakes region with Robert La Salle, founding Ft. Crèvecoeur (near Peoria, Illinois) in 1680. They were captured by Sioux Indians and taken to a site Hennepin named the Falls of St. Anthony (later Minneapolis); after four months they were rescued. Hennepin returned to France in 1682 and wrote about his adventures.

Father Marquette Is Chosen to Go with Jolliet

How exactly Father Jacques Marquette came to accompany Jolliet is a mystery. Perhaps Jolliet remembered Father Marquette's ambitions to convert the Illinois and other tribes who lived along the river from when they had met at Sault Ste. Marie. Perhaps Father Dablon recommended him to Talon because Marquette got along with the Indians and had a talent for learning their languages and dialects.

During France's early colonial period, it was common for a priest to accompany a dangerous voyage. He would protect the explorers' souls and bless them if they were on the brink of death. The presence of Father Marquette was also a symbol of the partnership between the Catholic Church and the government of New France. Talon knew that the Jesuits were anxious to explore the great river, but he wanted to limit their power. By having a priest join the expedition, the government could maintain their authority over the Church because Jolliet, the leader of the expedition, represented the government.

Jolliet and Marquette did not embark on their journey alone. Jolliet recruited trading partners who were up for the adventure and whatever profits could be made. From the very beginning, the voyage was purely a business venture. Except for Marquette and Jolliet, the voyagers had pelts and profits on their minds. Jolliet and seven other Frenchmen signed a contract that gave Jolliet one-half of the trade profits and the remaining partners one-seventh of the other half of the profits. Jolliet's younger brother, Zacharie, and a longtime business partner of Jolliet's, François de Chavigny, invested in the trip, but did not come along. Zacharie had to stay at Sault Ste. Marie to take care of the family fur business. Jacques Tiberge, Pierre Largilier, Pierre Moreau, Jean Plattier, and Pierre Porteret went along for the trip, but did not invest any money in it.

4

ON THE WAY TO
THE GREAT RIVER

*As we were going to seek unknown countries, we took all pos-
sible precautions, that if our enterprise was hazardous, it
should not be foolhardy: for this reason we gathered all possible information from Indians who had frequented those parts,
and even from their accounts traced a map of all the new
country, marking down the rivers on which we were to sail, the
names of the nations and places through which we were to
pass, the course of the great river, and what direction we
should take when we got to it.*
—From Father Marquette's narrative in Shea's *Discovery and
Exploration of the Mississippi Valley*, published in 1852

In May 1673, Jolliet and his five companions
set off from Sault Ste. Marie to pick up Father
Marquette on the north shore of Lake Huron.
Since 1671, Father Marquette had been working
at the mission of St. Ignace helping to develop the
settlement of the Michilimackinac tribe. They
traveled three to a canoe and paddled four miles
per hour in smooth water. The birch-bark canoes
were strong and light. They were designed so
that they would be easy to carry. The crew
would have to be ready to throw the
canoes on their shoulders and walk

This 1672 painting shows Father Marquette and Louis Jolliet traveling by canoe with Native Americans down the Mississippi River. Marquette drew a map of the country through which they passed and kept a diary of the voyage. This diary, with its clear, concise style, is one of the most important and interesting documents of North American colonial history.

around parts of the river that weren't navigable by boat, where it was too narrow or shallow, where there were waterfalls or violently churning rapids, or where there were too many islands.

Marquette and Jolliet's expedition was quite well-prepared, especially in comparison with the La Salle expedition that had gone before them. La Salle set off blindly and somewhat arrogantly in his quest for the Great River of the West, without taking any advice from the native peoples. La Salle did not know how to speak Algonquian or Iroquoian, the two major languages of the North American Indians. He did not even know how to follow a compass. Needless to say, he got lost many times.

These are some pieces of Native American jewelry. Native Americans greatly prized the beads that Europeans traders exchanged with them for furs.

Unlike La Salle, Marquette and Jolliet didn't underestimate the power of the wilderness while preparing for their voyage. They wanted to take as many precautions as possible. They brought Indian corn and dried meat to last the entire trip, and presents for the Indians to show the tribes that they were coming in peace. They brought guns and gunpowder to hunt with, and ink and paper to take notes with. Most important, though, they brought a rough map of the region they would travel through. All through the previous winter, Jolliet had stopped every Indian who had wandered through Sault Ste. Marie and asked for information about the lands and tribes that the expedition would encounter. Then, he pieced together a map from the information he gathered.

On May 17, 1673, with all of their supplies in the canoes, Jolliet, Marquette, and their fellow travelers pushed off from St. Ignace. They paddled through part of Lake Huron and the Lake of the Illinois and made their way to the Bay of the Fetid, now Green Bay. They were two weeks into their journey when they met the Wild Oats Nation, or the Menominees. They were called the Wild Oats Nation by the French because they survived on the wild oats that grew in abundance in the marshes around them.

The Menominees Tell the Frenchmen Not to Go On

The Europeans told the Menominees that they intended to continue exploring down river. Father Marquette mentioned that he wanted to find distant tribes and instruct them in the ways of his religion, and Jolliet said that he was planning to find and follow the Great River of the West to see where it ended. The Menominees didn't want them to go. They told the Europeans that they were bound to get themselves killed if they went further. Indian nations farther south tomahawked strangers and there was the danger of being killed. They also said that the Great River was a danger in itself: It was full of river monsters that swallowed up men and canoes. The Menominees came up with one reason after another to keep the Europeans from going on.

While it's possible that they had a genuine interest in the well-being of the explorers, the Menominees may have also wanted to protect their own interests. After all, from their point of view, Europeans were a nuisance: They wanted to change

Chief Grizzly Bear of the Menominee tribe is pictured in this painting. He was their leader nearly 150 years after Marquette and Jolliet first encountered the tribe. The Menominees lived in the Upper Peninsula of Michigan in an area that stretched south to Illinois and west to Minnesota. After the French annexed the lands of the Great Lakes region by a formal act at Sault Ste. Marie, all Indian tribes of the area were declared French subjects, thus consolidating the fur trade.

the Indians' lives, and they interfered with normal trading patterns between the tribes. If the Europeans continued exploring down the river, they would establish direct trade relationships with tribes farther south. It was possible that the Menominees were acting as middlemen and were trading with the Europeans on behalf of tribes farther south. They might have tried to keep the Frenchmen from going because they did not want to lose their privileged position.

Marquette, Jolliet, and their fellow Frenchmen did not suspect the Menominees of lying. They laughed at the Indians' superstitions and continued with their journey from the southern foot of the Bay of the Fetid into the lower Fox River. Of course, because they were still in territory that was familiar to the French, it was easy for them to not take the Indians' warnings seriously. Even though they had never been to that area themselves, other Frenchmen had. In fact, they were about to come upon St. Xavier, another Jesuit mission. Once they reached lands that no white man had ever set foot upon, it would become harder to ignore the Indians' warnings.

As the small group left the Bay of the Fetid behind and entered the Fox River, they were in awe of the natural beauty of the landscape. Father Marquette watched the waves of the bay slap against the shore and wondered where the tides came from. Did they rise and fall

Father Marquette and Louis Jolliet saw many beautiful scenes of nature on their journey.

with the moon? Or was it the wind that pressed on the center of the lake? He noticed that the wild oats at the mouth of the Fox River attracted bustards, ducks, teal, and many other birds. On their way along the upper Fox River, Father Marquette picked an herb known for being a remedy against snakebites. His friend Father Allouez had told him to be on the lookout for it. An Indian had once revealed the secret power of the herb to Father Allouez in a series of ceremonies. Many of the Indians honored the healing powers of nature, especially if it was so great that it guarded against death.

49

The Town of Maskoutens

After examining the natural beauty, the French arrived at Maskoutens, a town on a small hill surrounded by stretches of prairie scattered with groves of tall trees. Three nations, the Maskoutens, the Miamis, and the Kiskabous lived there together. As the explorers entered the town, Father Marquette was encouraged by the sight of a cross planted in the middle of town. The cross was draped with white pelts, red belts, and bows and arrows that the Indians offered to their god, the Great Manitou, in thanks for giving them plenty of game during the winter and keeping them from starving.

The Frenchmen knew that a river that emptied into the Mississippi lay three leagues west-southwest of Maskoutens, but they needed help finding it. After giving the Maskoutens, Miamis, and Kiskabous gifts, the explorers asked if they could spare some guides. The Indians agreed to help, and on June 10, 1673, two Miami guides departed with the expedition. They led the Frenchmen across marshes and lakes covered with wild oats to the Meskousing, or what is now known as the Wisconsin River. They had finally reached the end of their known world. From the beginning of their voyage they had relied on the knowledge of other Frenchmen, but now they had no one to rely on but themselves. The real adventure began the moment the explorers left their Miami guides and put their canoes into the Wisconsin River.

5

MEETING THE ILLINOIS

Two carried tobacco–pipes well–adorned, and trimmed with many kinds of feathers. They marched slowly, lifting their pipes toward the sun, as if offering them to him to smoke, but yet without uttering a single word. They were a long time coming the little way from the village to us. Having reached us at last, they stopped to consider us attentively. I now took courage, seeing these ceremonies, which are used by them only with friends, and still more on seeing them covered with stuffs, which made me judge them to be allies. I, therefore, spoke to them first, and asked them, who they were; they answered that they were Illinois, and in token of peace, they presented their pipes to smoke.
—From Father Marquette's narrative in Shea's *Discovery and Exploration of the Mississippi Valley*, published in 1852

At the mouth of the Meskousing River, Jolliet and Marquette entered the Mississippi. Paddling in their canoes, they wove their way around beautiful islands, finding high mountains at first, and then flat land filled with animals such as the wildcat and the buffalo—wildlife that they had never seen before. In the river, they discovered new fish, including an enormous catfish that banged against the canoe and threw the explorers off-balance.

Fishing for catfish on the Mississippi River is still a popular activity. Catfish got their name from the long barbs, or feelers, on their mouths (they resemble cat whiskers). There are about 2,500 species of catfish, and most species live in freshwater. Freshwater catfish live in a variety of habitats, from stagnant water to fast mountain streams. Catfish are generally bottom dwellers and feed on almost any kind of animal or vegetable matter. As a meal, catfish are bony but very tasty.

As they went farther down the river, the explorers began to get nervous because they did not see any signs of human life. They couldn't ask anyone if they were going in the right direction and, at the same time, they were always afraid of a surprise attack. At night, they anchored far from the banks and slept in their canoes to protect themselves. Someone always stayed up during the night and guarded the sleeping, floating camp.

The explorers started out on May 17, 1673, and arrived at the Mississippi about three weeks later. They spent about a week bracing themselves for an encounter with unknown tribes. Finally, they spied footprints and a path that led to a prairie. Marquette and Jolliet were sure that it led to a village, so they left their companions and followed the path. The two men crept up on the village and hid until they had the courage to announce their presence. When they heard them, the Indians rushed out of their cabins. Four old men came forward to greet Marquette and Jolliet. The Indians may have recognized them as Frenchmen because of Marquette's black robe. The Indians called the French Jesuits "black robes" because of the way they dressed. The Indians told the Europeans that they were Illinois, and then two of the older tribesmen offered Marquette and Jolliet their pipes to smoke. This was the first time the explorers experienced the important Indian custom of smoking the calumet, or peace pipe.

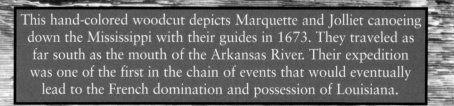

This hand-colored woodcut depicts Marquette and Jolliet canoeing down the Mississippi with their guides in 1673. They traveled as far south as the mouth of the Arkansas River. Their expedition was one of the first in the chain of events that would eventually lead to the French domination and possession of Louisiana.

The Illinois Welcome the French

In his narrative, recounted in John Gilmary Shea's *Discovery and Exploration of the Mississippi Valley*, Father Marquette wrote that he and Jolliet were taken to a cabin where an unclothed Illinois man waited for them, his arms outstretched toward the sun, "as if he wished to screen himself from its rays." The Illinois man exclaimed, "How beautiful is the sun when you come to visit us! All our town awaits thee, and thou shalt enter all our cabins in peace." It helped that the Illinois spoke a language that was similar to Algonquian. This made it easier for Jolliet and Marquette to communicate with the Illinois. In a formal ceremony, Marquette and the sachem, or chief of the village, exchanged presents and speeches. Marquette said that he and Jolliet came in peace to visit nations on the river. Marquette said he was sent by God, the creator of all of them, so that all of the nations could know Him. Either Marquette or Jolliet told the Illinois that the chief of the French had conquered the Iroquois. Then they begged the Illinois to tell them everything they knew about the sea.

It was then the sachem's turn to make a speech. He put his hand on the head of a little Illinois boy and said, "I thank thee, Blackgown, and thee, Frenchman, for taking so much pains to come and visit us; never has the earth been so beautiful, nor the sun so bright, as it has been to-day; never has our river been

56

The first Indians Marquette and Jolliet encountered on the Mississippi were the Illinois, who were friendly to the explorers because they needed guns and assistance against the Iroquois. The Illinois received them warmly and provided them with a peace pipe (calumet) to use for the remainder of the journey. The calumet represented the god of peace and war, and those who carried one were said to be able to travel unharmed through enemy lands.

so calm, nor so free from rocks, which your canoes have removed as they pass; never has our tobacco had so fine a flavor, nor our corn appeared so beautiful as we behold it to-day. Here is my son, that I give thee, that though mayst know my heart. I pray thee to take pity on me and all my nation. Thou knowst the Great Spirit who has made us all; thou speakest to him and hearest his word: ask him to give me life and health, and come and dwell with us, that we may know him."

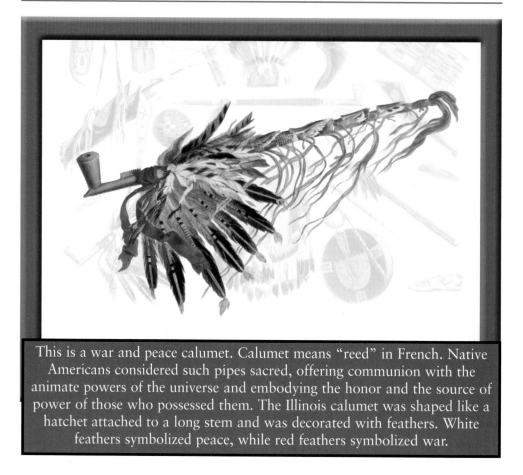

This is a war and peace calumet. Calumet means "reed" in French. Native Americans considered such pipes sacred, offering communion with the animate powers of the universe and embodying the honor and the source of power of those who possessed them. The Illinois calumet was shaped like a hatchet attached to a long stem and was decorated with feathers. White feathers symbolized peace, while red feathers symbolized war.

The sachem gave Marquette and Jolliet the little boy, whom they took as a sign of alliance between them, and a calumet which Marquette said they valued more than the boy. The calumet was a pipe that was said to have supernatural powers. The Illinois had a calumet for war, which had red feathers, and a calumet for peace, with white feathers. They gave Marquette a peace calumet and explained that it guarded against enemies. According to them, you could walk through a battle with it and your enemies would lay down their weapons.

At the end of his speech, the sachem begged the explorers not to go any further on their trip because it was too dangerous. Then, the council of the Illinois and the two explorers sat down to a feast. They ate sagamity, an Indian porridge, as well as fish and a piece of buffalo. The Illinois offered the Frenchmen a large dog as a third course, but Marquette and Jolliet politely told them that they didn't eat dog.

Later on in the evening, the Illinois led them around the whole village so that everyone could see the Europeans and give them tokens of their respect. The Frenchmen visited 300 cabins and, according to Marquette, received belts, garters, and other articles made of the hair of bear and buffalo, dyed red, yellow, and gray. The next day, they left the village and headed downstream despite the sachem's warnings. They promised to return for a visit on their way back up the Mississippi River.

The Ways of the Illinois

During the expedition's short stay, Father Marquette gathered a lot of information about the Illinois. Marquette found out that the word "Illinois" meant "the men." In his journal, Marquette wrote that the Illinois seemed more human than the other tribes who seemed more like "beasts" to him.

This engraving shows Native Americans harvesting a crop of maize, or corn. Maize was the predominant staple of the Indian communities of the eastern part of the present-day United States. Almost all other foods were mixed with corn gruel or baked in little corn cakes.

There were several different villages of Illinois, many spaced so far apart from one another that they spoke different versions of the same language. The men hunted and went to war. The Illinois women did everything else: They prepared the ground for planting, sowed the seeds, harvested the corn, and pounded it into cornmeal. They also built wigwams and carried them on their shoulders when they traveled to trade or hunt at different hunting grounds. Wigwams were dome-shaped or oval huts made out of woven mats and hides that were sewn together to keep out rain.

In his narrative, Marquette said that the Illinois men had a habit of taking many wives and cutting off their noses or ears if they were unfaithful. The Illinois also took slaves from different tribes. They traded animals and furs for European guns, so that they could easily intimidate tribes to the west of them who had never had contact with the Europeans. They decorated their faces for war with red lead and ochre-colored soil, and the chief wore a special belt made out of bear or buffalo hair; colorful arm, knee, and wrist bands; and rattles made of deer hoofs that he tied below his knees.

Marquette was impressed with Illinois culture, especially the calumet dance, which he compared to a European ballet. He promised the Illinois he would return to teach them about Christianity on his way back up the Mississippi.

6

THE POWER OF
THE PEACE PIPE

We heard from afar the Indians exciting one another to combat with continual yells . . . some young men sprang into the water to come and seize my canoe, but the current having compelled them to return to the shore, one of them threw his war-club at us, but it passed over our heads without doing us any harm. In vain, I showed the calumet, and made gestures to explain that we had not come as enemies. The alarm continued, and they were about to pierce us from all sides with their arrows, when God suddenly touched the hearts of the old men on the water side, doubtless at the sight of our calumet.

—From Father Marquette's narrative in Shea's *Discovery and Exploration of the Mississippi Valley*, published in 1852

The band of explorers coasted down the Mississippi and witnessed marvelous paintings of what they thought were monsters so high up on the rocks that it was hard to believe that anyone could have reached that high to paint them.

This hand-colored woodcut shows Marquette and Jolliet waving good-bye to the Illinois Indians, who had made an alliance with the Europeans. Marquette is shown with an Illinois calumet, with its traditional red and white feathers, in his hand.

Soon after, they heard the rapids of the muddy Pekitanoui (what is now known as the Missouri River) rushing into the Mississippi from the northwest. Jolliet hoped that it might lead to the Gulf of California because by now he knew that if the Mississippi continued south, it would empty into the Gulf of Mexico.

Going Through the Rapids

Marquette and Jolliet heard from the Indians that it was possible to follow a series of rivers to a sea, which was assumed to be the Gulf of California.

The Rock Paintings on the Cliffs

Marquette wrote that the rock paintings were "as large as a calf, with horns on the head like deer, a fearful look, red eyes, bearded like a tiger, the face somewhat like a man's, the body covered with scales, and the tail so long that it twice makes the turn of the body, passing over the head and down between the legs, and ending at last in a fish's tail." He made a sketch of the petroglyphs, but that sketch is now lost.

Marquette and Jolliet descend the Mississippi in this engraving. As they went further down the river, they grew more and more convinced that it flowed into the Gulf of Mexico, and not the Pacific. Nevertheless, they decided to continue on their journey.

The explorers canoed south about twenty leagues to the Ouaboukigou River, which is now called the Ohio River. They had to pass a small bay filled with twenty-foot-high rocks and whirling rapids that the Indians had warned was a dangerous spot. The tribesmen told them that a *manitou*, or demon, lived there. The Frenchmen maneuvered around the rocks and came to cliffs that were veined with iron ore. They also found purple, violet, and red earth that stained one of the canoe paddles for fifteen days.

As they moved south, the landscape and climate gradually began to change. Cane and then cotton-wood and elm trees lined the banks. And quails and parakeets appeared. The hot sun and the mosquitoes began bothering them, so they made a cabin out of their sails on top of the canoes.

Marquette and Jolliet Encounter the Chickasaws

Indians soon appeared on the riverbanks and threatened them with guns. Marquette saw that they were dressed like the Huron and tried to speak Huron with them. The Indians turned out to be Chickasaws. They had guns, axes, hoes, knives, beads, and glass bottles, which they had gotten from Europeans. When the two groups figured out a way of communicating, the Chickasaws told the Frenchmen that they traded with Europeans who had rosaries (prayer beads) and pictures, and lived on the eastern side of the Mississippi. They also told them that they were only ten days from the sea. Marquette and Jolliet must have realized that the Europeans the Chickasaws were referring to were Spaniards. The Frenchmen continued traveling south. They were excited by how near the sea was and hoped the Spaniards were far east of them and out of their way.

The expedition soon came across the village of the Michigamea. These Indians

66

Spanish explorers ride behind Native American guides. The French and the Spanish explored the North American continent from opposite directions. The Spanish moved up from the South and the French moved down from the North. Their conflicting ambitions led to much hostility.

were on the verge of attacking them. They were brandishing their bows, arrows, axes, and war clubs on the riverbanks, and some were paddling out in canoes to surround them, when Father Marquette presented the calumet. When the Michigamea saw it, they put their weapons down. Marquette used sign language to communicate with the Michigamea and gain information about the next village. The next day, they went down river to the village of the Akamsea, or Arkansas, Nation with a canoe full of Michigamean men and a Michigamean interpreter.

This painting shows Father Marquette preaching. Marquette recorded in detail the villages and customs of the different tribes he met, the topography of the countryside, the tides of the lakes, the future commercial value of navigable streams, and the variety of the flowers, trees, birds, and animals he saw.

The chief of the Akamsea came toward them in a canoe holding a calumet. A young Akamsea man knew the Illinois dialect, so the Michigamean interpreter was not needed. Father Marquette preached to them about the Christian god and then they asked the Akamsea about the sea. The Akamsea told the Frenchmen that they were only ten days from it, but that they did not know who lived down there. Their enemies would not let them go south toward the sea. Marquette and Jolliet found out that the Akamseas' enemies were the Chickasaws—the Indians with guns that Marquette and Jolliet encountered earlier.

The Great Spirit

Manitou was the Indian word for "spirit." The Indians called their god the Great Manitou, or Great Spirit. Each person had a private manitou that watched over him or her like a guardian angel. In their sleep, the Indians dreamed of a specific animal such as a bird or snake, which symbolized their manitou. They prayed to it when they needed luck with wars, fishing, and hunting. The Indians also called bad spirits manitous. Special places in nature, like waterfalls and caves, also had manitous. They made offerings to their manitous to honor them or to ask favors.

The red line on this modern map shows the route Marquette and Jolliet traveled in their journey down the Mississippi River.

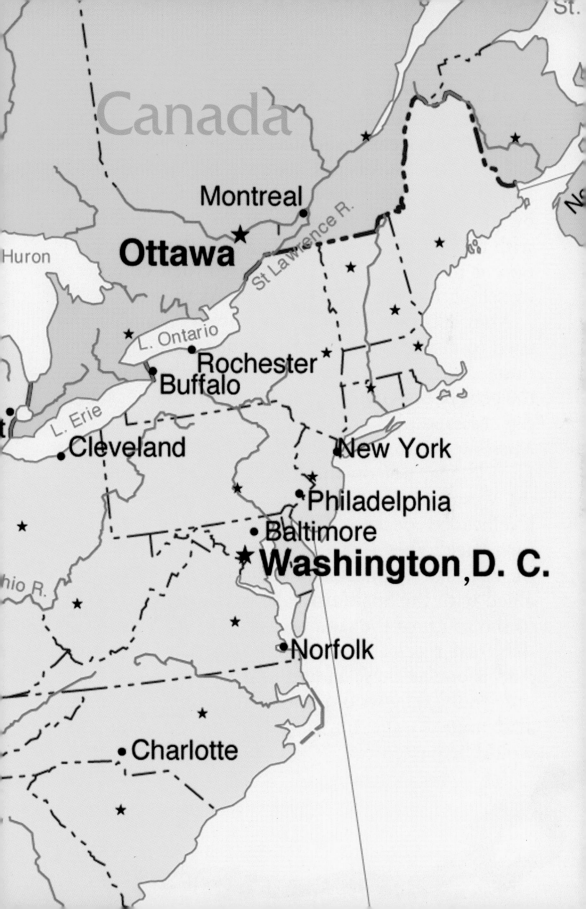

The Chickasaws continually threatened the Akamsea because they did not want them to trade with the Europeans who lived down by the sea. This is how the Chickasaws reduced their competition and got a higher price for their animal hides. Also, by preventing the Akamsea from trading directly with the Europeans, the Chickasaws kept their position as middlemen. They increased their commerce by selling European goods to the Akamsea.

Marquette and Jolliet stayed with Akamsea and tried to decide whether or not they wanted to continue south. On July 17, 1673, they had achieved the goal of the voyage, which was to find out where the Mississippi emptied. They knew that the Mississippi emptied into the Gulf of Mexico, or Florida Sea, not on the East Coast in Virginia, or the West Coast in California. The explorers made a levelheaded decision. They cautiously agreed to turn back. They did not want to risk their lives at the hands of Spaniards, or Indian nations who were allied with the Spaniards. All of the Indian nations to the south of the Akamsea would have guns that they had received by trading with the Spaniards. And if one of these Indian villages happened to be unfriendly, they would not only lose their lives, but also none of the information they had gathered would be passed on.

7

THE RETURN VOYAGE

My Lord,
It is not long since I am back from my voyage to the Sea of
the South. I was favored by good fortune during the whole
time, but on my return, when I was about to reach Montreal,
my canoe capsized . . . I lost consciousness, and after four
hours in the water, I was found by fishermen who never go to
this place and who would not have been there if the Blessed
Virgin had not obtained for me this grace from God, Who
stayed the course of nature in order to rescue me from my
death. Except for this shipwreck, Your Excellency would have
had a quite interesting relation, but all I saved was my life.
  —From a 1674 letter from Jolliet to Louis de Baude, comte
              de Frontenac, as it appears in Virginia Eifert's
                           biography of Louis Jolliet

Marquette and Jolliet were wise to turn back while they still felt fresh. This way they avoided conflict with Spaniards and conserved their energy for the return trip. They had traveled 1,100 miles from the mouth of the Wisconsin River to the mouth of the Arkansas River, and they had every reason to feel a sense of accomplishment. However, the remainder of the journey would be

much more difficult. Even though they were familiar with the territory because they had already passed through it, now they would have to contend with the strong Mississippi current. Because of the current, it would take them twice as much energy and time to get back. They would try to paddle against it when they could, but often, especially when they came across rapids, they would have to get out of the water and carry the canoes.

Leaving the Akamsea

The Marquette and Jolliet expedition left the Akamsea on July 17, 1673. They went as far as the rock paintings, then turned east up what is now known as the Illinois River. They were following a shortcut that Marquette had heard about from Father Allouez. The fertility and beauty of the land surrounding the river impressed the explorers. Throughout their whole voyage, they had seen nothing like it. The prairies attracted every kind of wildlife, from buffalo and swan to parrot and beaver. They sailed sixty-five leagues up the river until they reached the friendly village of the Kaskaskia, who were part of the Illinois.

This is a painting of Marquette's home on the Chicago River as it looked in 1673. That same year, Indians directed Marquette and Jolliet to Lake Michigan via the Chicago River. The two explorers learned that the Indians of the region called the area around the mouth of the river Checaugou, after the wild garlic (some say onions) that grew there.

The Kaskaskia delighted Father Marquette when they asked him to return to their village and instruct them in the teachings of Christianity. Father Marquette promised to come back and fulfill his dreams of setting up a mission among the Illinois. He decided that he would name his future mission after the Immaculate Conception. Jolliet also dreamed of coming back to this country. He wanted to settle a colony in the mild climate that was not as cold as New France, and not as hot as the mosquito-infested South.

One of the Kaskaskia chiefs and a few young men led Marquette and Jolliet from their village to the Lake of the Illinois (now known as Lake Michigan). On their way, Father Marquette passed a few roaming Peoüarea Indians, who also belonged to the tribe of the Illinois. He preached to them and also baptized a dying baby. In his writings, he said that he was happy to have come all that distance just to have the certainty of saving one soul.

The St. Xavier Mission

At the end of September 1673, the expedition arrived where it had started—at the St. Xavier Mission on the Bay of the Fetid. Although there are no records of the expedition's return, the exhausted travelers probably returned to a mission that was deserted.

It was autumn and time for the hunting season, so the Indians would have been off in the woods looking for deer and bear. The priests who usually lived at the mission would have been gone, too, having followed the Indians to their hunting grounds.

Marquette and Jolliet parted ways after reaching the mission. Marquette stayed at the mission and planned his next trip to visit the Illinois. Jolliet went back to Quebec. Their voyage had been a success. They had achieved their goal of finding out where the Mississippi ended, and they had all arrived home safely and in good health, which in itself was quite a feat. No one had drowned or died of disease, and they had completely avoided being attacked by Indians.

Marquette and Jolliet did have one piece of bad news to relay to the authorities: The Great River of the West did not empty into the Gulf of California. Nonetheless, Marquette was happy; after all, he had his mission among the Illinois. However, Jolliet could not help but feel a little disappointed, especially after the excitement of the journey was over. Not only had he failed to solve the mystery of the Northwest Passage, but he had also failed to bring back furs. Now that he was home, he owed his trading partners money.

Many of the waterways in New France were whitewater rapids, making accidents and drownings quite frequent. In this engraving, two men struggle to save their lives and the lives of their horses after their canoe strikes a fallen tree along a river.

Disaster Strikes

Things got worse for Jolliet: His canoe capsized on his way back to Quebec. Jolliet set out from Sault Ste. Marie in the spring of 1674 with two men and an Indian boy. He paddled down the St. Mary River to Lake Huron, past the mission of St. Ignace where Father Marquette used to work, to the Ottawa River. The Ottawa River was whirling with recently melted snow. In the Lachine Rapids near Montreal, the canoe hit a rock and threw all of the contents of the canoe, including the Indian boy and the men, into the water. Jolliet was lucky that a few fishermen were out that day. Usually, they did not fish in the rapids because it was too hard to catch fish in the rough water. But that July of 1674, the fishermen saved Jolliet's life; they dragged him out of the water before he drowned.

Jolliet was devastated. He had lost everything except his life in the accident. The Indian boy and his traveling companions were killed and Jolliet's map and journal of his discoveries along the Mississippi disappeared in the rapids. Jolliet had to walk into Quebec without a single piece of proof of where he had been. As he expected, no one in Quebec cared about his exploration of the Mississippi. The only people who paid any attention to him were those who wanted the profits of his business venture.

This hand-colored woodcut depicts the death of Father Marquette. After turning back from the Mississippi, Marquette had planned to preach among the Illinois who had earlier treated him so kindly. After spending only three weeks with them, he became troubled by failing health and left for Sault Ste. Marie. He contracted dysentery on the way and died in the woods off Lake Michigan. He was nearly thirty-eight.

Jolliet continued to hope that he would be recognized for his exploration. He had a copy of his map and journal at the warehouse in Sault Ste. Marie, and if he could only get it, he could show Frontenac, the governor of New France, all of the waterways that could possibly lead to the Gulf of California. After all, the French had not yet explored where the western tributaries of the Mississippi came from. At the beginning of August, though, terrible news from the western frontier dashed Jolliet's only surviving hope. The warehouse at Sault Ste. Marie burned down. He had to completely redraw his map and rewrite his notes from memory. Father Dablon, the superior of Jesuits in New France, helped him remember details by asking him questions.

Marquette Returns to the Illinois

While Jolliet was suffering much embarrassment in Quebec, Father Marquette was trying his best to get back to his Illinois mission among the Kaskaskia. He had grown weak and was often sick with fevers, chills, and diarrhea. The journey down the Mississippi had worn him out. He had to wait until he was healthier and stronger before he could leave. Finally, on October 25, 1674, Father Marquette left with two men who had been with him and Jolliet throughout the Mississippi voyage. The group persevered through snow and icy winds, but then Marquette fell sick again and was unable to go on. The Frenchmen decided they had no choice but to spend the winter between the Chicago and Des Plaines Rivers. At the end of March, they set out for the Illinois village and at last reached their destination on April 10, 1675. Father Marquette stayed through Easter Sunday and preached to the willing listeners. On his way back to St. Ignace, he died in the wilderness near what is now Ludington, Michigan. It was May 17, 1675, and he was just shy of turning thirty-eight years old. He had just fulfilled his promise to the Illinois.

Many historians now believe that Father Dablon wrote Marquette's narrative after Marquette died. Dablon rewrote Marquette's journal from Marquette's notes and inserted details that he had collected from his conversations with Jolliet in Quebec.

8

JOLLIET'S LIFE AFTER THE MISSISSIPPI

His majesty is unwilling to grant the leave asked by the Sieur Jolliet to go to the Illinois Country with twenty men in order to begin a settlement there. The number of settlements could be increased before thinking of settlements elsewhere; this should be your guiding principle in regard to newly made discoveries.
—From a letter to Louis Jolliet from Jean-Baptiste Colbert, the colonial minister

The same year that Father Marquette's life ended, Jolliet's began anew. He married Claire-Françoise Bissot, a daughter of family friends. She was nineteen years old and he was thirty. Jolliet settled down in Quebec and joined the family fur-trading business, and Claire-Françoise became pregnant. Jolliet attended trade fairs with the Indians. Business was slow and fewer Indians came to the trading post than before. Jolliet wondered if the English were luring them away with better offers, or if the coureurs du bois had gotten to them first and had already traded with them. The little daily contact that he had with the Indians made him want to go out into the wilderness himself. He was torn between his duty to stay home with his family and his desire to leave.

This is a 1992 photograph of Louis Jolliet's home in Champlain, Quebec. After the voyage with Marquette, Jolliet traveled up the Saguenay and Rupert Rivers in 1679 to spy on the British positions around the Hudson Bay. As a reward, he received Anticosti Island. In 1694 he made another journey, exploring the coast of Labrador and visiting the Eskimos. He died in 1700 when he got lost on a trip to one of his land holdings.

Jolliet Asks to Go to Illinois Country

Remembering the beauty of the Illinois country, Jolliet asked the new intendant, Jacques Duchesneau, if he could start a colony there. Duchesneau asked the colonial minister, Colbert, on behalf of Jolliet, but Colbert rejected the request. To make matters worse, Jolliet had to watch as the government of France gave the explorer Robert La Salle almost exactly what they had denied Jolliet. In 1678, La Salle was granted permission to start a colony and build a fort and ships along the Illinois River. This would allow France to expand its power and establish a trading route between the big lakes in the North and the Gulf of Mexico at the bottom of the Mississippi.

The same spring that Jolliet was rejected, he learned of Marquette's death and burial in the wilderness around the Lake of the Illinois. While he was extremely sad that his friend had died, he was glad that Marquette had been able to return to the Illinois. It was a bittersweet time for Jolliet.

Being a man of action, and not one to sit and sulk after being rejected, Jolliet threw himself into family life. He and Claire-Françoise had a second child, and Jolliet starting caring for his young wife's brothers and sisters. He

After Marquette and Jolliet's successful exploration of the upper Mississippi River, Robert La Salle took another expedition there and claimed the river for the French. He was given a grant to establish a colony there, and was accompanied by Louis Hennepin, who drew maps of the region.

enjoyed teaching them lessons at home because he could not afford to send them all to school. It was during this time of domestic happiness that Jolliet began to receive recognition for his exploration of the Mississippi. In 1679, the government granted him the Mingan Islands along the northern bank of the St. Lawrence east to the Lance aux Espagnols Bay, which is now known as Brador Bay. This gave him the right to set cod and seal fisheries along the northern coast of the Gulf of St. Lawrence.

Jolliet Spies for His Country

In 1679, Intendant Duchesneau sent Jolliet north to Hudson Bay. His goal was to scope out what exactly the English were doing in that area. Pelts were trickling into Quebec, and the French had to figure out a way to open up the fur trade in the North. Jolliet and his crew paddled through dark, brooding cliffs of the Sanguenay to the tundra region and made their way to an English fort on the southern bank of the Rupert River.

Jolliet met with Charles Bayly, the governor of the Hudson Bay Company, and learned that the English had many ships that cruised up rivers of the bay region to trade with the Indians. The English also had three more forts and were pushing west along the rivers that emptied into Lake Superior. They had taken over all of the French fur trade along these rivers. The English had a better trading strategy than the French. They traveled to the Indians to trade with them instead of making the Indians come to them.

As they talked, the governor became more and more taken in by Jolliet's charm. He knew Jolliet's reputation as an expert mapmaker and explorer

This woodcut depicts the Hudson Bay Company trading store in upstate New York. The Hudson Bay Company began in 1670 as a simple fur-trading enterprise and evolved into a trading, exploration, and land development company with vast holdings in the Canadian provinces; a merchandising, natural resources, and real estate development company; and, today, Canada's oldest corporation.

and wanted to recruit Jolliet for his own purposes. After he informed Jolliet of the plans of the English to go farther west, he asked Jolliet to work for him. He needed a capable man who could go far west and set up a fort among the Assiniboin Indians, who had the best beaver pelts. Jolliet was shocked. The governor was asking him to become a traitor to his country. Being a loyal Frenchman, Jolliet immediately refused the governor's offer. He could have easily supported his growing family with the money the governor offered him, but the money meant nothing compared to the shame he would have felt if he betrayed his king and country.

In 1680, the king of France and the government of New France thanked Jolliet for serving his country by giving him Anticosti Island at the mouth of the Gulf of St. Lawrence. The island had 2.5 million acres of beautiful scenery and wildlife and it was very well situated. Every ship coming into the St. Lawrence River had to first pass Anticosti. Anticosti was too cold to live on during the winter, but in the summers, Jolliet could bring his family there. He could also use the island for hunting and lumber, and the surrounding waters were well-suited to setting up more seal and cod fisheries.

On November 2, 1693, Jolliet petitioned the government to explore the coast of Labrador. Over the preceding few years, his property on Mingan and Anticosti had been raided and looted by the English. He could not fund the voyage alone, so he asked the government for help. He wrote, "Had it not been for two serious losses inflicted on me by the English, I would have followed up this discovery, but unless the Court gives me some assistance, it is useless for me to think about it." The government allowed Jolliet to go, but once again, they would not finance the expedition.

This time, Jolliet did not feel as if he was taking such a great risk. His friend François Viennay Pachot gave him most of the supplies he would need. And it had been his experience that, although the king was reluctant to invest money in the beginning, he always rewarded his explorers with generous land grants and cash once an explorer could prove he was successful.

Meeting the Eskimo

On April 28, 1694, Jolliet and his three oldest sons, Louis (eighteen), Charles (sixteen), and François, (fifteen), pushed off for Eskimo land. They took along a crew of eighteen, including a priest. They sailed north out of the St. Lawrence River along the Gaspé Peninsula and stopped at the Mingan settlement to get supplies and say good-bye to the rest of the family. The ship crept north and hugged the rocky shoreline as Jolliet looked for the mouths of rivers to map.

On his expedition to the north, Jolliet met Eskimos like the ones pictured here. This painting is a copy of one made by the explorer John Ross of three of his Eskimo friends, Shulanina *(left)*, Tulluachiu *(center)*, and Tirikshiu *(right)*.

They passed through the Strait of Belle Isle between Newfoundland and the Labrador coast and swung out into the Atlantic Ocean. At one point the Jolliets thought they saw a crowd of white ships anchored ahead, but upon closer inspection realized that these were massive icebergs. Pieces of the icebergs crashed into the water. When Jolliet heard this explosive sound, he thought that the English might be attacking. A day later, they came upon their first Eskimos, who were rowing toward them in a sealskin canoe. The French and the

Eskimos traded with and sang songs to each other, but otherwise, it was difficult to communicate. One of the only words Jolliet learned was one they repeated often: *tcharacou*, which means "peace."

When Jolliet returned in August 1694, he presented his navigation map of the St. Lawrence River to Frontenac, who passed it on to King Louis XIV. Later on, Jolliet opened a school of hydrography in Quebec and became professor of hydrography. In 1700, he left the school to summer on Anticosti Island with his family. No one knows how he died, but he never came back to Quebec after that summer. Jolliet was fifty-five when he passed away. A memorial service was held September 15, 1700, in the Cathedral of Notre Dame in Quebec.

9

MARQUETTE AND JOLLIET: THEIR LEGACY

I, René–Robert Cavelier de La Salle, by virtue of His Majesty's commission, which I hold in my hands, and which may be seen by all whom it may concern, have taken and do now take, in the name of his Majesty and his successors to the crown, possession of the country of Louisiana, the seas, the harbours, ports, bays, adjacent cities, towns, villages, mines, minerals, fisheries, streams, and rivers, within the extent of the said Louisiana.

—Robert La Salle, 1682

Jolliet's heroic achievements became well-known not only in New France, but in France and England, too. Marquette became famous shortly after he died because his description of the voyage survived him. The famous French cartographer Franquelin drew a map of Jolliet and Marquette's discoveries and published it alongside the journal that Dablon rewrote. The book came out in Paris in 1681, under the title

This memorial plaque is in Louis Jolliet's garden at his home in Quebec. Jolliet and Marquette are memorialized not only in Canada, but also throughout the midwest United States in the names of colleges, towns, and roads.

Voyage et Découverte de Quelques Pays et Nations de L'Amerique Septentrionale, which means the "Voyage and Discovery of a Few Countries and Nations of Southern America." Marquette and Jolliet made important progress in the history of European exploration, and yet when we mention explorers of the Mississippi, the names Marquette and Jolliet aren't usually the first to come to mind.

In the mid 1500s, the Spaniard Cabeza de Vaca was on his way to the Gulf of California when he first came across the Mississippi. In fact, the Indians who lived near the river forced de Vaca and his men into slavery on an island off the coast of the Mississippi. As the legend goes, the Spaniards eventually escaped, but the Indians from the villages that they passed thought they were supernatural beings and made the Spaniards their medicine men. Another Spanish explorer, Hernando de Soto, is usually given credit for being the first to discover the Mississippi, in 1541. In a desperate search for gold, he crossed the river, which he called the Rio Grande de Espiritu Santo—the Great River of the Holy Spirit. He died soon after and was buried in its waters. Many Spanish explorers, including Francisco Coronado, had either seen the Mississippi briefly or heard about it.

Marquette and Jolliet may not have been the discoverers of the Mississippi, but they were the first Europeans to truly explore it. They canoed down a great length of it, from the mouth of the Wisconsin River to the mouth of the Arkansas River. They never got to experience the joy of reaching the end of the Mississippi, of smelling the muddy waters of the river mixing with the salt water, and of finally sailing out into the open waters of the Gulf of Mexico. It was Robert La Salle who did this.

In 1682, La Salle pushed down to the delta from the head of the Illinois River. He boldly claimed the Mississippi, its tributaries, and all the land around it for the king of France. He named the territory Louisiana after King Louis XIV. France would have never benefited from Marquette and Jolliet's exploration if La Salle had not come along and formally taken possession of the land. La Salle had made the French presence in the Mississippi Valley official. But without the previous discoveries of Marquette and Jolliet, La Salle would have never been able to reach the end of the Mississippi and claim the surrounding territory for France. The Marquette and Jolliet expedition was the first link in a chain of events that eventually led to France's possession of the Louisiana Territory.

Not only did Marquette and Jolliet contribute to the expansion of the French colonial empire, but they also contributed to our knowledge of the ways in which different Indian tribes and nations lived. The way of life among the Maskoutens, Miamis, Kiskabous, Illinois, Chickasaws, Akamseas, and Michigameas has changed dramatically over the years, but the eye-witness accounts of the French explorers as written by Father Dablon help us reconstruct their past practices.

This map shows the territory the United States acquired in the Louisiana Purchase. France sold the western half of the Mississippi River basin, about 828,000 square miles (2,144,520 square km), for the equivalent of less than three cents per acre. It was the greatest land bargain in U.S. history. The purchase doubled the size of the United States, greatly strengthened the new nation materially and strategically, and provided the means for westward expansion and development.

CHRONOLOGY

1627 Cardinal Richelieu organizes the Company of the One Hundred Associates.

1637 Jacques Marquette is born in Laon, France.

1645 Louis Jolliet is born in Quebec, New France.

1663 King Louis XIV gets rid of the Company of the One Hundred Associates and declares New France a crown land under his control.

1666 Jacques Marquette is sent to Quebec by Jesuit authorities.

1668 Louis Jolliet goes to France to study cartography and hydrography.

1669   Daniel de Remy, sieur de Courcelle, the governor of New France, sends out the first French expedition in search of the Great River of the West.

1669   Louis Jolliet goes west and joins his brother in the fur trade at Sault Ste. Marie.

1669   Jacques Marquette leaves Sault Ste. Marie for the mission of Saint-Esprit.

1671   Daumont de Saint-Lusson takes formal possession of the West for Louis XIV and France in Sault Ste. Marie.

May 17, 1673   The Marquette-Jolliet expedition starts its journey at St. Ignace.

June 10, 1673   Jacques Marquette and Louis Jolliet enter the Mississippi River at the mouth of the Wisconsin.

July 17, 1673   The Marquette-Jolliet expedition leaves the Akamsea near the mouth of the Arkansas River and turns back up the Mississippi.

1674   Louis Jolliet's canoe capsizes and he loses his journal and map of the expedition.

May 17, 1675 Jacques Marquette dies.

1680 France recognizes Louis Jolliet for his achievement by giving him Anticosti Island.

1682 Robert La Salle takes possession of the Mississippi Valley for France.

1700 Louis Jolliet dies.

GLOSSARY

bustard A game bird that lives on dry, grassy plains.

capsize To overturn or upset a boat.

cartography The making of maps.

colonist A settler of a new country; an inhabitant of a colony.

colony A foreign territory taken into possession by a monarch or in the monarch's name.

delta A tract of land, often more or less triangular in shape, enclosed or traversed by the diverging mouths of a river.

ell An old unit of measurement which varied in different countries from twenty-seven to forty-five inches.

fishery The business, occupation, or industry of catching fish or other products from seas, rivers, and other bodies of water, or the regions where the fish are caught.

frontier   The part of a country held to form the border or furthest limits of its settled or inhabited regions.

gross   A quantity equal to twelve dozen.

hydrography   The mapping of bodies of water.

iron ore   Any native compound of iron from which the metal may be profitably extracted.

Jesuits   A religious order of Catholic priests founded by St. Ignatius Loyola to spread the faith among unbelievers.

league   An inexact, old unit of measurement, usually about five kilometers or three miles.

marsh Low-lying land that is flooded in wet weather and is usually watery at all times.

medicine man   The name for a healer among North American Indians.

mission   The act of being sent out by the church to convert unbelievers. Can also be a place where conversion takes place.

missionary   A person sent out on a religious mission.

sieur A title of respect in French, like "sir" or "lord" in English.

teal A short-necked, freshwater duck.

tributary A stream or a river flowing into a larger river.

tundra A vast, nearly level, treeless Arctic region, usually with a marshy surface and permanent underfrost.

wampum Beads made from the ends of shells, rubbed down, polished, and threaded on strings, worn by Indians as a decoration or used as a form of currency.

FOR MORE
INFORMATION

In the United States

Father Marquette National Memorial
Upper Peninsula Travel and Recreation Association
P.O. Box 400
Iron Mountain, MI 49801
(800) 562-7134
Web site: http://www.nps.gov/fama

Wisconsin Historical Society
816 State Street
Madison WI 53708
(608) 264-6400

The University of Iowa Museum of Natural History
10 Macbride Hall
Iowa City, IA 52242
    (319) 335-0480
      Web site: http://www.uiowa.edu/~nathist

In Canada

Canadian Museum of Civilization
100 Laurier Street
P.O. Box 3100
Station B
Gatineau, PQ J8X 4H2
(800) 555-5621
Web site: http://www.civilization.ca/

Web Sites

Due to the changing nature of Internet links, the Rosen Publishing Group, Inc., has developed an online list of Web sites related to the subject of this book. This site is updated regularly. Please use this link to access the list:

http://www.rosenlinks.com/lee/jmlj/

FOR FURTHER READING

Bohlander, Richard E. *World Explorers and Discoverers*. New York: Macmillan Publishing Company, 1992.

Bogue, Margaret Beattie. *Around the Shores of Lake Michigan: A Guide to Historical Sites*. Madison, WI: University of Wisconsin Press, 1995.

Clark, James I. *Wisconsin: Land of Frenchmen, Indians, and the Beaver*. Madison, WI: State Historical Society of Wisconsin, 1959.

Donnelly, Joseph P. *Jacques Marquette, S. J., 1637–1675*. Chicago: Loyola University Press, 1968.

Eifert, Virginia. *Louis Jolliet: Explorer of Rivers*. New York: Dodd, Mead, & Company, 1961.

Lurie, Nancy Oestreich. *Wisconsin Indians*. Madison, WI: State Historical Society of Wisconsin, 1980.

Scanlon, Marion. *Trails of the French Explorers*. San Antonio, TX: Naylor Company, 1956.

BIBLIOGRAPHY

De Voto, Bernard. *The Course of Empire*.
   Boston: Houghton Mifflin, 1952.
Donnelly, Joseph P. *Jacques Marquette, S. J.,
   1637–1675*. Chicago: Loyola University Press, 1968.
Eifert, Virginia. *Louis Jolliet: Explorer of Rivers*.
   New York: Dodd, Mead, & Company, 1961.
Shea, John Gilmary. *Discovery and Exploration of the
   Mississippi Valley: With the Original Narratives of
   Marquette, Allouez, Membré, Hennepin, and
   Anastase Douay*. New York: Redfield, 1852.
Sparks, Jared. *American Biography*. New York:
   Harper Brothers, 1902.

INDEX

About the Author

Tanya Larkin is a freelance writer living in New York.

Photo Credits

Cover, p. 4 © N. Carter/North Wind Picture Archives; pp. 9, 20, 32, 36, 43, 88 © Bettmann/Corbis; pp. 11, 13, 24, 28–29, 39, 44, 54–55, 57, 60, 63, 80–81, 85, 87, 95 © North Wind Picture Archives; p. 14 © Gianni Dagli Orti/Corbis; p. 17 © National Gallery Collection, by kind permission of the Trustees of the National Gallery, London/Corbis; p. 23 © Arte & Immagini srl/Corbis; pp. 27, 78 © Corbis; p. 35 © Archivo Iconografico, S.A./Corbis; p. 46 © National Museum of Art, Washington, D.C./Art Resource; p. 49 © Academy of Natural Sciences of Philadelphia/Corbis; p. 52 Dover Pictorial Archive; p. 58 © Historical Picture Archive/Corbis; pp. 65, 68 © Culver Pictures; pp. 67, 98 © Hulton/Archive/Getty Images; pp. 70–71 © MapArt; p. 74 © Baldwin H. Ward and Kathryn C. Ward; p. 92 © Mary Evans Picture Library.

Series Design

Tahara Hasan

Layout

Les Kanturek

Editor

Annie Sommers